PLAYING SMARTER TENNIS

Tips to Win More Points & Have More Fun!

PETER M. ENGSTROM, USPTA

Illustrated by: Marcus Fort

BALBOA.PRESS

A DIVISION OF HAY HOUSE

Balboa Press books may be ordered through booksellers or by contacting:

Balboa Press
A Division of Hay House
1663 Liberty Drive
Bloomington, IN 47403
www.balboapress.com
844-682-1282

Print information available on the last page.

ISBN: 978-1-9822-7792-5 (sc)
ISBN: 978-1-9822-7791-8 (e)

Balboa Press rev. date: 01/04/2021

CONTENTS

FOREWORD

Tennis: A Game of Errors

Tennis is a game of errors. While the statistics change from match to match, in general:

- About 30% of the points are outright *winners*. These are shots that the opponent does not touch before the ball bounces twice. (I suspect you knew that!) An untouched serve is called an ace. But winners are also realized with good groundstrokes, offensive lobs, volleys, and drop shots.
- The remaining 70% of the points won result from *forced* errors and *unforced* errors. The classification of the type of error is typically a judgment call on the statistician's part and their perception of the player's skill.

Forced errors are those balls that are touched by the opponent but not successfully returned. Here the result is attributed to the skill of the player who won the point.

Unforced errors, on the other hand, are those shots that were expected to be returned by the Receiver but were not. They were either hit into the net, hit wide, hit long, or mishit.

This general ratio seems to be true regardless of the level of play.

Recognizing the above, where can you have the most significant influence to win more points?

There is nothing you can do about your opponent's skill level. But you can attempt to reduce your number of unforced errors and minimize your opponent's opportunities to hit winners by playing smarter tennis.

I trust the tips offered herein will provide you with some tactics and practices you can use to:

- have more time to prepare for your return shot
- be in the best court position to return your opponent's ball
- make your opponent's return of your shot more difficult
- feel more confident about your level of play
- stay in the point longer, and in so doing, give your opponent the chance to make an error. (Wouldn't that be nice!)

INTRODUCTION

About this Book

There is a wealth of tennis instruction books available that teach you how to hit each stroke properly. This is not one of them.

Instead, it assumes you have a fundamental understanding of basic stroke production and are currently playing recreational tennis for fun and exercise.

If you are among this group, this booklet is for you. It shares what I hope are some valuable tips on:

- Stroke selection
- Playing strategy
- Court position
- Court movement

Collectively they are aimed at helping you:

- serve more effectively
- play with more confidence

- make fewer unforced errors
- stay in the point longer
- approach the net more effectively
- successfully poach
- intimidate your opponent(s)
- bring out the best in your doubles partner.

I trust they will introduce some playing fundamentals and suggestions that will be of value each time you get on the court and ultimately enable you to:

- win more points, and
- have more fun.

So, let's get started with Chapter 1: Make the Court Your Friend.

CHAPTER 1

Make the Court Your Friend

1. Using Net Height to your Advantage

The net is admittedly the most critical structure on any tennis court. It is the main obstacle of the game and is responsible for making the game exciting and challenging.

We can all agree that hitting the ball over the net is essential to successfully playing the game. A player's skill, quickness, and power mean nothing if the ball doesn't go over the net and into the opponent's court.

In your enthusiasm to smash the dickens out of the ball and crush your opponent, you may never have taken the time to appreciate the subtleties of the net structure.

According to International Tennis Federation rules, the net is supported between two 3½ foot tall posts located 3 feet outside the double's sidelines. (Similarly, 3½ foot portable support posts are placed 3 feet outside the singles sidelines for singles play.)

These supports result in a net approximately 42 inches high at the sideline for singles and doubles play. ITF rules also require a net height of 36 inches at the center. (Note the convenient adjustable center strap!) Hence, the net is 6 inches lower at the center than at the sideline!

(Please see Figures 1.1)

Figure 1.1
Official Net Height*

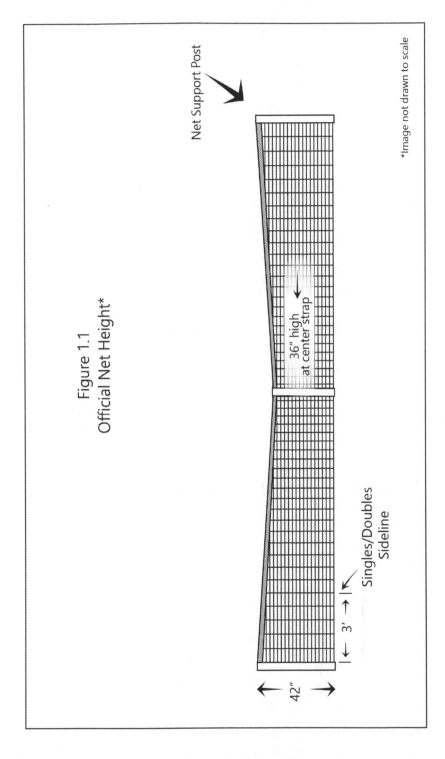

Net Support Post

36" high
at center strap

Singles/Doubles
Sideline

3'

42"

*Image not drawn to scale

How can I use this to my advantage, you ask?

Tip 1:	**If you want to increase your chances of successfully hitting the ball over the net, hit over the center of the net.**

For example, suppose you decide to hit a killer groundstroke down the sideline for a sure winner. Unfortunately, your ball hits 2 inches below the top of the net and drops unceremoniously into your court for an unforced error. (Bummer!)

Had you hit your return over the center of the net, it would have cleared the net by almost 3 inches! While it may or may not have been a sure winner, it would have kept you in the point.

Please recognize we are not advocating that you hit every shot over the center of the net. We are only pointing out that doing so will increase your chances of getting the ball over the net (objective number one in tennis). And, even better, it will give your opponent a chance to make an error. (Wouldn't that be fun?)

2. Using Net Clearance to Your Advantage

Often beginner or intermediate players, especially those who hit with little or no topspin, tend to hit their groundstrokes low over the net to avoid going long. (Sounds like a good idea, doesn't it?)

Unfortunately, while hitting the ball low over the net may increase your chances of keeping it from going long, it decreases your margin for error. Often such a low shot ends up hitting the net, pitifully dropping in your court for an unforced error.

Tip 2: **To reduce the possibility of such errors, *aim* your groundstrokes to pass at least 18 inches over the top of the net.**

Doing so will reduce the possibility of an unforced net error. And it allows you to hit the ball deeper into your opponent's court, making it more difficult for them to approach the net. (Making it harder for your opponent to come to the net is always a good strategy.)

If you hit *flat* returns with little or no topspin, remember to take some pace off your shot so that it does not land behind the baseline.

(Please see Figures 1.2)

Figure 1.2
High vs. Low Over-the-Net Trajectories*

High Trajectory
(At least 18" over net)

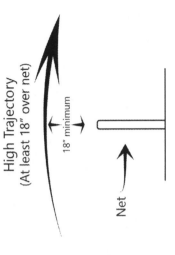

18" minimum

Net

Note: Higher trajectories will reduce unforced net errors. In addition, they land deeper in your opponent's court making it difficult for them to approach the net.

Low Trajectory
(Perhaps 6-8" over the net)

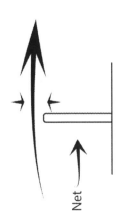

Net

Note: Hitting only a few inches over the net increases chances of making net errors. In addition, such low shots land shorter in the opponent's court ... inviting them to take the net and hit subsequent winners.

*Image not drawn to scale

6

3. Using Court Dimensions to your Advantage

As you know, the singles tennis court measures 27 feet wide by 78 feet long. If you take a moment to apply high school geometry to these dimensions (remember the Pythagorean Theorem), you quickly realize that the singles court diagonal length (corner-to-corner) is 82½ feet or 4½ feet longer than the straightaway court length!

Adding the two 4½ foot doubles alleys increases the width of the doubles court to 36 feet. This extra width results in a doubles court diagonal length of 85.9 feet - almost 8 feet longer than the straightway court length! (Nice to know if you tend to hit your straightaway shots long!)

(Please see Figures 1.3 and 1.4)

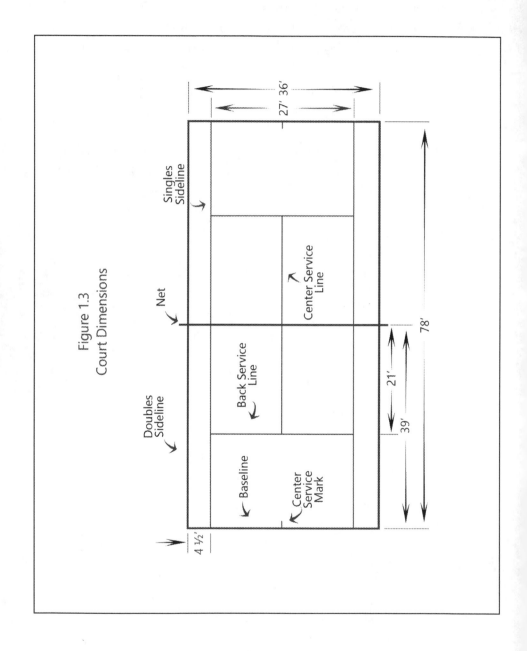

Figure 1.3
Court Dimensions

Singles Sideline

Center Service Line

Net

Doubles Sideline

Back Service Line

Baseline

Center Service Mark

27' 36'

78'

21'

39'

4 ½'

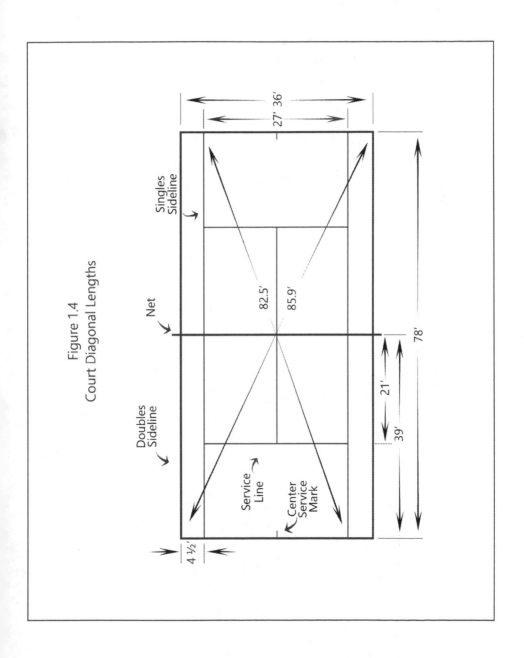

Figure 1.4
Court Diagonal Lengths

This extra crosscourt length (thank you, Pythagoras) leads us to our next tip:

Tip 3: **To reduce your *long* unforced errors (hitting the ball beyond the baseline), take advantage of this extra length by hitting your groundstrokes crosscourt.**

For example, a ball hit straightaway from the singles court righthand corner that was out by a foot would have been in by more than 3 feet had it been hit crosscourt. A ball hit straightaway from the doubles court righthand corner that flew out by 5 feet would have been in by almost 3 feet had it been hit crosscourt.

(Please see Figure 1.5)

Figure 1.5
Straightaway Error vs. Crosscourt In-Play

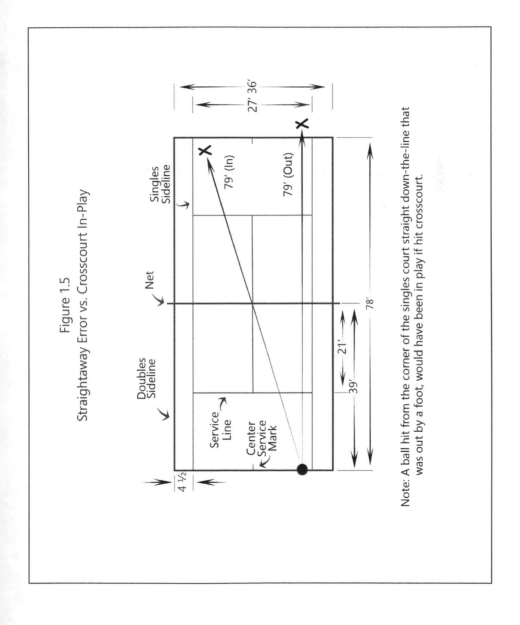

Note: A ball hit from the corner of the singles court straight down-the-line that was out by a foot, would have been in play if hit crosscourt.

Who wouldn't want to take advantage of this knowledge and its possibilities?

Hitting your groundstrokes crosscourt also allows you to use the lower portion of the net, giving you:

- **a higher probability of avoiding an unforced net error,**
- **the chance to pull your opponent out of position and,**
- **the opportunity to hit with a little more pace while still keeping the ball in play.**

So why not *make the court your friend* by taking advantage of the lowest portion of the net and the extra length provided when you hit crosscourt.

CHAPTER 2

Playing the 'Zones' ... with Purpose

In this chapter, I would like to share some thoughts about playing strategy depending upon where you are on the court. To do so, let us divide the court into three *zones*.

The *Defensive* Zone: the court area around and behind the base line up to the service line. This area includes the court section popularly called *No Man's Land*. (More about this later.)

The *Offensive* Zone: the court area from the service line to about 6 to 8 feet from the net.

The *Kill* Zone: the remainder of the court to the net.

Please accept that these "zones" do not have absolute dimensions. Instead, they are relative areas from which defensive, offensive, and put-away (or *kill*) shots respectively are hit.

(Please see Figure 2.1)

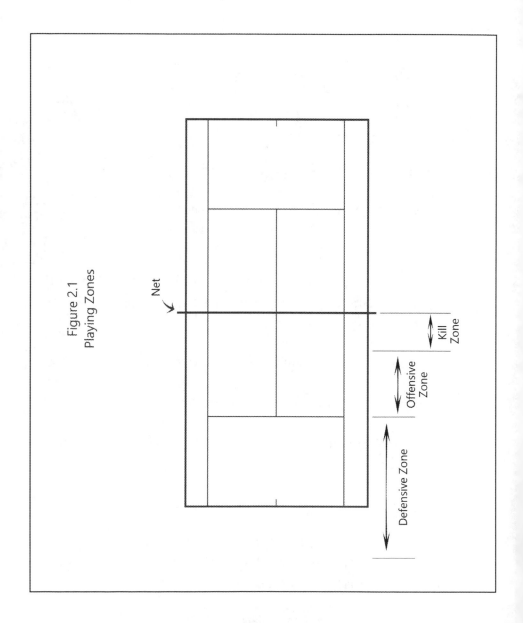

Figure 2.1
Playing Zones

Playing in the *Defensive Zone*

This zone is so named because when hitting from here, you have:

- the fewest angles with which to hit your return, and
- the least opportunity to hit a clean winner.

(This, of course, is not necessarily true for advanced players with exceptional control, topspin, pace, and a perfected drop shot/ topspin lob - e.g., Rafael Nadel, Roger Federer, et al.).

However, for the beginner or developing intermediate player, hitting from this zone is primarily a defensive effort. (Hence its clever name).

From this zone, your goals are:

- to return the opponent's shot into their court, allowing them a chance to make an error.
- to keep your opponent in their defensive zone -away from the net where they cannot cause you much trouble.
- to stay in the point until you have an opportunity to hit a winner from the baseline, approach the net to play offensively, or until your opponent makes an error. (Oh, boy!)

To achieve these goals, we encourage revisiting the tips provided in Chapter 1 to avoid some of those nasty and disappointing unforced errors:

Tip 1:   **Hit over the lowest part of the net.**

Doing so will reduce your net errors and give you a slightly longer court for your return shot to stay in play.

Tip 2: **Aim your return high, at least 18 inches, over the net.**

Doing so will eliminate some net errors.

Also, we encourage you to:

Tip 3: **Attempt to keep the ball deep in your opponent's court to make it difficult for them to approach the net. (Hitting high over the net will help achieve this).**

(Please see Figure 2.2)

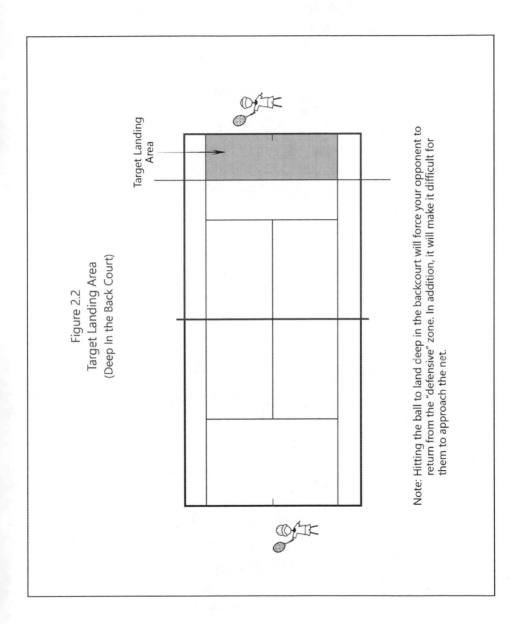

Figure 2.2
Target Landing Area
(Deep in the Back Court)

Target Landing Area

Target Landing Area

Note: Hitting the ball to land deep in the backcourt will force your opponent to return from the "defensive" zone. In addition, it will make it difficult for them to approach the net.

Tip 4: **Use the defensive lob (high and deep) when you need to *buy time* because you find yourself out of position or to drive your opponent back away from the net**. (More about this in Chapter 6.)

Nothing is more frustrating for an aggressive net player than being pushed back into the court's defensive zone after they have worked their way up to the net.

Please recognize that playing from the baseline can be great fun, especially when playing against someone who is not comfortable coming to the net or who enjoys hitting the dickens out of the ball from the baseline.

After all, long rallies are much more fun than running around retrieving balls that lie ignominiously on the court due to unforced errors after only two or three hits.

Playing in the *Offensive Zone*

Unlike *No Man's Land* (Chapter 3), the Offensive Zone is a desirable place. It is so named because you can play more offensively from here – and possibly win more points.

From this area of the court you:

- have more angles within which to hit a winner.
- can hit a mid-court volley - giving your opponent less time to set up for their next return and possibly forcing an error. (Yea!!)
- are in a better position to make an offensive approach shot. You can then close on the net into the Kill Zone for an easy put-away volley. (Wouldn't that be fun!)

- may have the chance to hit an overhead smash - if your opponent puts up a short lob. The overhead smash is one of the most fun shots in tennis and demoralizing for your opponent.

Unfortunately, to get to the *Offensive Zone*, you must pass through the dreaded *No Man's Land*.

Tip 5:	**Do not try to get to the Offensive Zone immediately after hitting a groundstroke from behind the baseline. It is a long way to go, with little time to get there and prepare for your next shot.**

Unless you are swift on your feet, there is not enough time to get to the offensive zone, stop, and set up before your opponent strikes their return. Instead, be prepared to stop in no man's land so you can react to your opponent's return. Make that return and then move up into the Offensive Zone. (More about this in Chapter 4 – "Approaching the Net.")

Tip 6:	**Wait until your opponent hits a short ball that brings you inside the baseline (into no man's land) to begin your approach to the net. Doing so will allow you to step into your return stroke, then quickly move into the Offensive Zone.**

Playing in the *Kill Zone*

This zone is so named because you have the best opportunities to hit a blistering *winner* from here. From this position, you have:

- the chance to hit a high volley (a relatively easy shot to master)

- the opportunity to shorten the amount of time your opponent has to prepare for and execute their return stroke (possibly causing them to make an error)
- an assortment of angles to hit your return for a clean winner. (That would be great fun!)
- the possibility of hitting the ball down towards the opponent's feet, making it hard for them to hit a return
- the opportunity to hit a winning volley down the middle of the court between your opponents. (A most enjoyable shot.)

One Last Note for Beginners:

It has been my experience that many beginning players are uncomfortable approaching the net. The easiest way to overcome this discomfort is to practice and master the volley.

Trust me. It is among the easier shots to master- especially in beginner or intermediate tennis, where the ball is hit at speeds well below those seen in tournament play. These slower speeds give you more time to prepare and hit a solid volley.

In the unlikely event you do get hit by the ball, it will not be painful. Just embarrassing. (Remember, the balls' covered with felt!) Once you get confident, you will find going to the net is great fun - and essential in competitive doubles play. (I believe you will learn to enjoy playing in the *kill* zone.)

CHAPTER 3

No Man's Land - the No Parking Zone

As mentioned in Chapter 2, *No Man's Land* is a portion of the defensive zone. Specifically, it is the area from a few feet inside the baseline to the service line.

(Please see Figure 3.1)

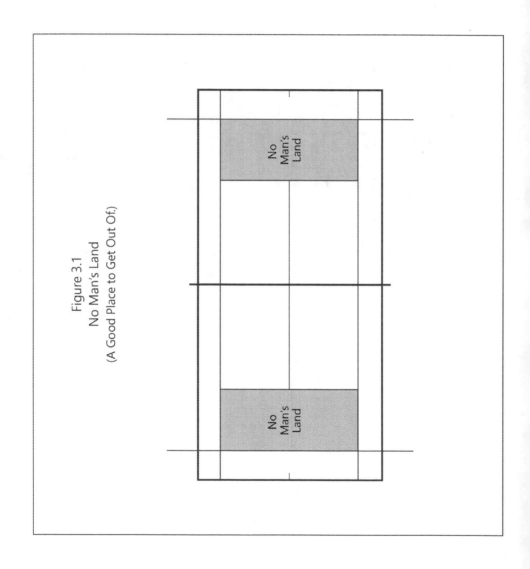

Figure 3.1
No Man's Land
(A Good Place to Get Out Of.)

The reason for its name is that it is not a good place to stand or hang out. In effect, it is a *No Parking* zone.

Why you ask! As you know, most good tennis players try to hit their returns to land deep in their opponent's court. Doing so helps keep your opponent out of the offensive zone (where you now know they would have a better chance to hit a winner.)

If you stand in No Man's Land, where will these deep returns from your opponent typically land? You got it. At your feet! (Ugh!)

When faced with a return that bounces at your feet, you generally have two, less than desirable, options:

- hitting a low volley, which you must hit "up" to clear the net. (Even if you manage to make this shot, it is like giving your opponent in the offensive or kill zone a birthday present. One which he is likely to turn into a winner. (You can only hope that they get too much blood in their eyes and mishit it!)
- hitting a half volley on the short hop. (This is generally a defensive shot and one that is difficult to master.)

For these reasons, it is a wise player who does not linger in No Man's Land for more than one shot – a shot typically necessitated by:

(1) a 'short' return which draws you over the baseline, or

(2) a 'weak' serve.

Both of these shots will pull you forward into the court (towards or into No Man's Land), where you can make your return after one bounce. Once there, you have the opportunity to be more aggressive as you move out of the Defensive Zone and into an offensive position.

Tip 1: **Take advantage of this *invitation* from your opponent. Move in to return the ball on one bounce. Then keep moving forward into the Offensive Zone for your next shot.**

Please let me say that again. Return the ball on one bounce *and* keep moving toward the net.

For those of you who are not yet comfortable moving to the net, I encourage you to resist the temptation to return to the comfort of the Defensive Zone for the following reasons:

(1) Depending upon the speed of play, you are likely to be *backing up* when your opponent returns your last shot. If so, your momentum will have you moving away from the net, causing you to hit your opponent's shot off your back foot. Doing so will usually result in an error or a weak return that invites your opponent to come to the net! (And, who wants that?)

(2) You will have wasted a perfect opportunity to make your next shot an offensive one – possibly even a *winner*. From the Offensive Zone, you can practice hitting your mid-court volleys or overhead smashes (if your opponent inadvertently puts up a short lob). Perhaps even a winner.

At a minimum, your opponent will have less time to prepare for their return and possibly make an unforced error.

(3) If you don't play the net once in a while, how will you ever get better at it?

(Please see Figure 3.2)

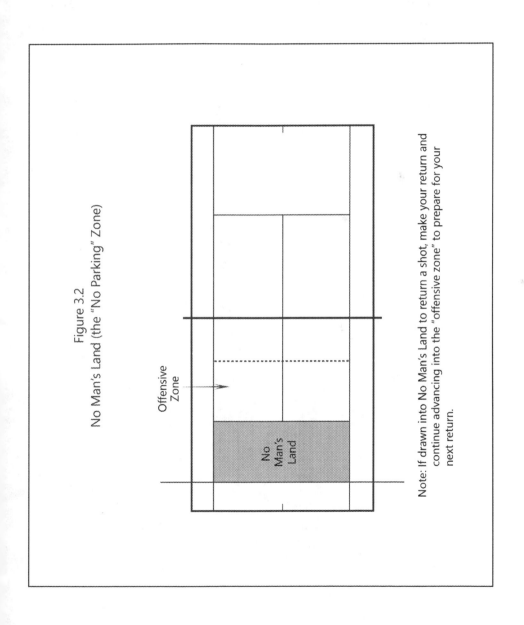

Figure 3.2
No Man's Land (the "No Parking" Zone)

Offensive Zone

No Man's Land

Note: If drawn into No Man's Land to return a shot, make your return and continue advancing into the "offensive zone" to prepare for your next return.

In the next chapter, we will discuss taking the net starting from the baseline, suggested footwork, and approach strategy. We'll have more tips for increasing your chances of returning the ball in play, staying in the point, and (of course) having more fun.

Rushing the Net

CHAPTER 4

Approaching the Net with Confidence

In Chapter 3, we reviewed how a weak serve or short return presents an invitation for you to take the offensive. Both situations force you to move into the court to return the ball on one bounce. Doing so puts you in the perfect position to move into the Offensive Zone for your next shot. Once here:

(1) You may be in a position to hit a winning volley.

(2) You may be able to hit a killer overhead smash.

(3) Your return will leave your opponent with less time to prepare for their next shot than they would have had if you were hitting from behind the baseline – possibly causing them to make an unforced error.

As your level of play improves and confidence increases, you may even decide to move toward the net after hitting a stroke from behind the baseline.

For example, perhaps:

- you have hit a defensive lob deep into your opponent's court that they most likely must return from behind the baseline (a defensive shot), or
- you have hit a deep groundstroke that your opponent may have to return from the Defensive Zone on the run.

Both of the above situations offer the opportunity to move forward into the offensive zone behind your approach shot.

Tip 1:	**When you decide to advance toward the net, do not run headlong at full speed to try to reach the kill zone. Instead, keep moving forward up to the point where your opponent is about ready to strike the ball. Before they do, make a *split-step* (see Figure 4.1).**

This split-step will stop your forward motion and put you on balance to react to your opponent's return depending upon its location. It allows you to step left or right to hit a volley or to turn sideways and shuffle (if needed) to hit an overhead smash.

(Please see Figure 4.1)

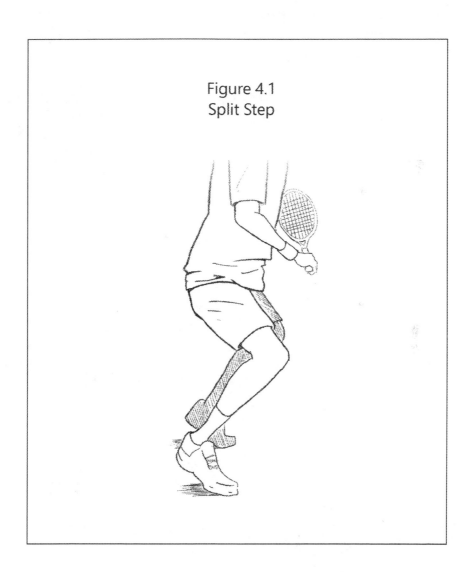

Figure 4.1
Split Step

Where to hit your approach shot:

Some suggestions for your approach shot placement:

Tip 2: Hit your approach down the nearest sideline (rather than crosscourt) and follow the flight of your shot as you approach the net.

(Please see Figure 4.2)

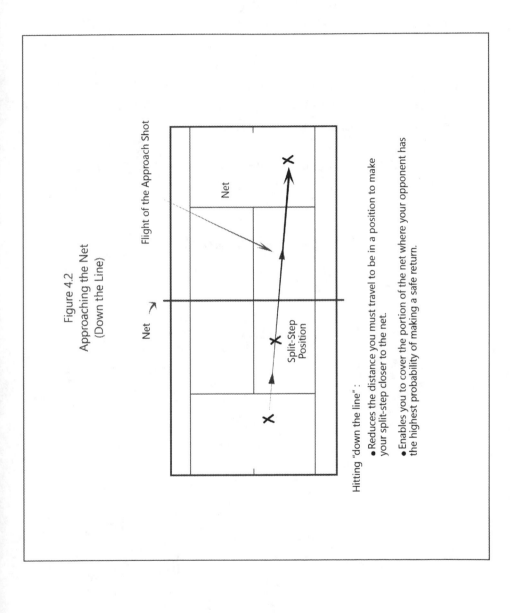

Figure 4.2
Approaching the Net
(Down the Line)

Net

Flight of the Approach Shot

Net

Split-Step Position

Hitting "down the line" :

- Reduces the distance you must travel to be in a position to make your split-step closer to the net.

- Enables you to cover the portion of the net where your opponent has the highest probability of making a safe return.

Shouldn't I be hitting over the lowest part of the net, you ask?

Not in this instance. Hitting a crosscourt return from your sideline position leaves your opponent with a huge open court into which they can hit an easy passing shot for a winner. (Rats@*&!).

Hitting down the line allows you to cover the portion of the net (about 2/3rds) that offers your opponent their best chance for a safe groundstroke. And it puts you in the best court position to reach your opponent's safer return.

And remember, when approaching the net, split-step before your opponent strikes the ball. Doing so will put you in a stable position to react to your opponent's return.

(Please see Figure 4.3)

Figure 4.3
Approaching the Net
(Crosscourt)

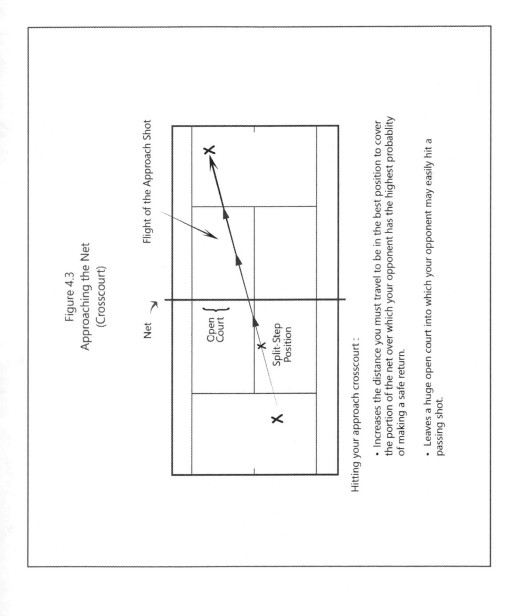

Net

Flight of the Approach Shot

Open Court

Split-Step Position

Hitting your approach crosscourt :

• Increases the distance you must travel to be in the best position to cover the portion of the net over which your opponent has the highest probablity of making a safe return.

• Leaves a huge open court into which your opponent may easily hit a passing shot.

CHAPTER 5

Serving with Advantage: Double Faulting is not a Sin!

The serve is undeniably the most important stroke in the game. If you cannot get the service into the service box, you cannot start the point! (And what fun is that!).

For many beginners and intermediate players, the pressure to do so results in many serves whose sole purpose is to start the point. To avoid faulting, their serves are often hit less aggressively or with little forethought about making it an offensive weapon.

Remember, the service is the only stroke in tennis over which the player has complete control. It is or should be an offensive shot. And, it should give the server an advantage with which to win their service games.

We would all like to serve at 100+ mph like Rafael Nadel or Serena Williams. Unfortunately, as recreational players, it is unlikely that we will ever develop the ability to realize such speeds.

However, there are some things that you can do to serve more offensively regardless of the pace with which you serve.

Tip 1:	Strive to get your first serve in play (regardless of pace).

Getting your first serve in play will give you an element of surprise, possibly causing your opponent to make an unforced error. (Lovely!)

Tip 2:	Strive to get your serve deep into the service box.

Doing so will force the receiver to return from deeper in their court, where they are typically on defense. Even a soft, looping service hit deep in their service box will take a high bounce making an aggressive return more difficult.

(Please see Figure 5.1)

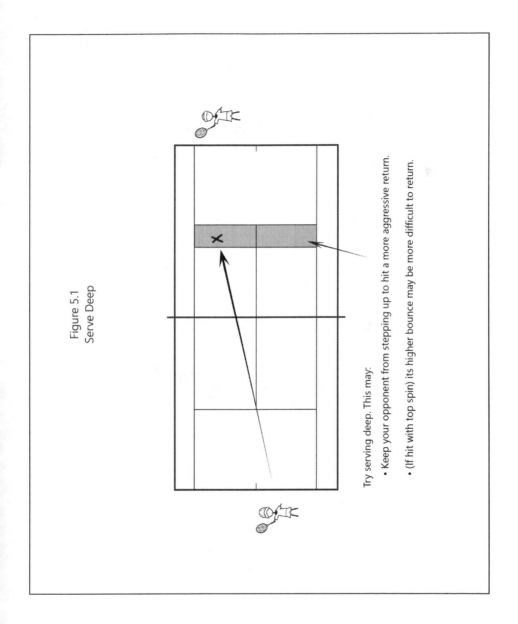

Figure 5.1
Serve Deep

Try serving deep. This may:

• Keep your opponent from stepping up to hit a more aggressive return.

• (If hit with top spin) its higher bounce may be more difficult to return.

Tip 3: **Do not hit every serve to the same general spot in the service box.**

If you can, try moving the service around. Serve to the receiver's forehand, backhand, and into their body. Moving the service around adds an element of surprise and keeps your opponent guessing! It will keep them off balance.

(Please see Figure 5.2)

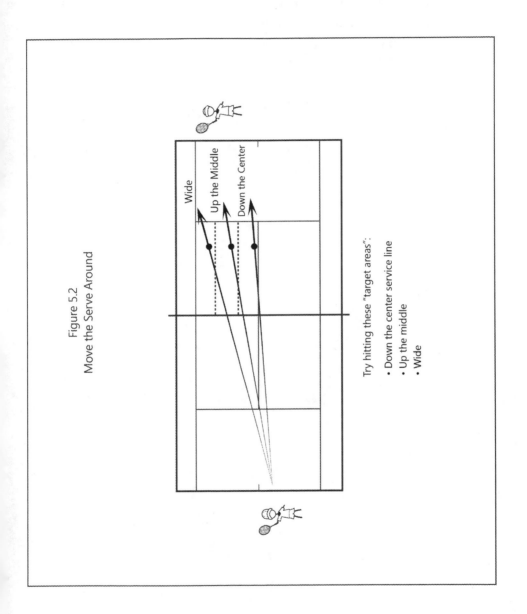

Figure 5.2
Move the Serve Around

Try hitting these "target areas":

• Down the center service line
• Up the middle
• Wide

| Tip 4: | **Exploit any perceived weaknesses** |

- If they have a weak backhand, try serving to their backhand.
- If they favor their forehand try hitting wide, forcing them to run to get their racquet on the ball. You may even hit a 50 MPH ace! (Now wouldn't that feel good.)

(Please see Figure 5.3)

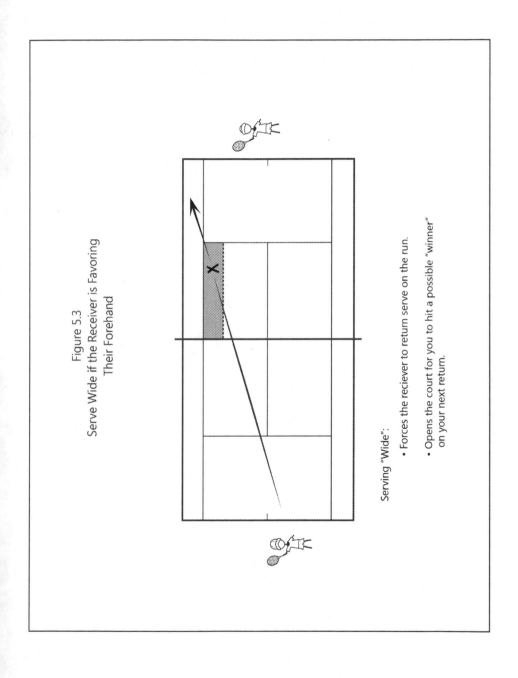

Figure 5.3
Serve Wide if the Receiver is Favoring
Their Forehand

X

Serving "Wide":

• Forces the reciever to return serve on the run.

• Opens the court for you to hit a possible "winner"
on your next return.

- If they are stepping into the backcourt hoping for a short serve, try serving deep into their body, perhaps causing them to make an unforced error.

(Please see Figure 5.4)

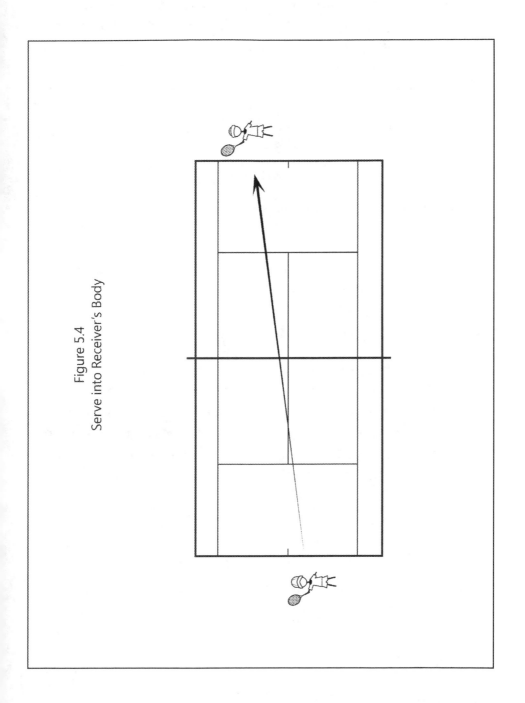

Figure 5.4
Serve into Receiver's Body

Tip 5: **Try hitting with the amount of pace with which you can consistently get at least 50% of your first serves in play.**

As you discover the pace with which you can achieve this, continue to use it. Eventually, you will increase your first serve percentage to a point where you may wish to try notching up your service pace a bit to again hit at least 50% of this more aggressive first serve in play.

Tip 6: **Double faulting is not a sin!**

Don't get discouraged if you double fault. An occasional double fault is OK. If you are not double-faulting occasionally, you are not aggressive enough on your serve.

Tip 7: **Practice! Practice! Practice!**

The service is the one stroke you can practice without a partner. Keep those old balls, and when time permits, take the bag or bucketful to an open court and practice. Experiment with pace and placement. You will be pleasantly surprised to find that, with good placement, you will win more points on serve. And, perhaps even hit an occasional ace! (Wouldn't that be nice?)

The Lob

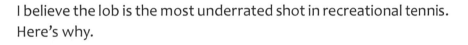

CHAPTER 6

The Power of the Lob

I believe the lob is the most underrated shot in recreational tennis. Here's why.

First, it is a relatively easy shot to make. It is hit with an open-faced racquet so that the ball travels high over the net. Consequently, there is no possibility of making a net error.

Second, it is hit for placement, not for pace or speed. Therefore, you typically have more control over the stroke with the benefit of keeping the ball in play.

Thirdly, it is a stroke that offers several possible ways to favorably affect your strategic position - with little possibility of making an unforced error. To better understand this, let us look at the two types of lobs at your disposal and their unique attributes.

Types of Lobs

Defensive Lob:

The defensive lob can be a useful tool in many situations. It is hit high over the head of the net player, preferably with sufficient depth to land deep in the backcourt.

(Please see Figure 6.1)

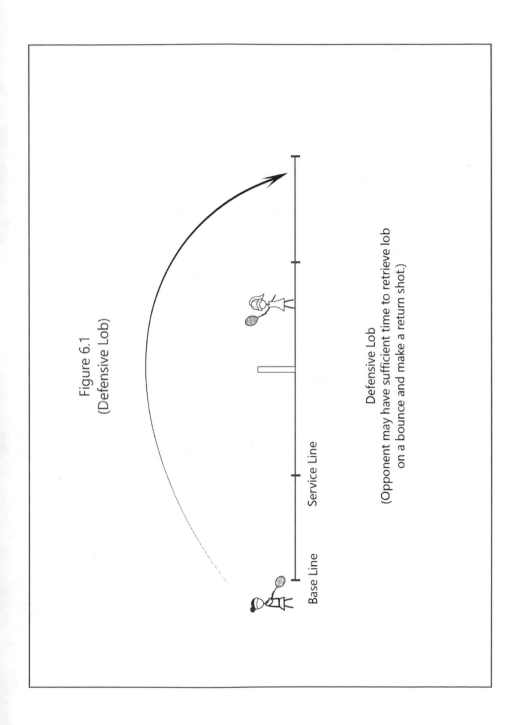

Figure 6.1
(Defensive Lob)

Base Line

Service Line

Defensive Lob
(Opponent may have sufficient time to retrieve lob
on a bounce and make a return shot.)

Among its many uses are:

(1) To take away your opponent's net advantage.

It is especially effective against opponents who like to come to the net. Lobbing high over their head forces them to return to the backcourt. Here, they are limited to hitting defensive returns - rather than offensive volleys or winning groundstrokes.

(2) To frustrate the aggressive net player.

Lobbing repeatedly during a point or a game can be extremely frustrating to your opponent. So much so that it breaks their concentration and can result in their hitting some unforced errors. (What a shame!)

(3) To tire your opponent.

Running back to retrieve a defensive lob and then trying to return it with some pace can be exhausting - especially if they must do so several times during the game or set. Such fatigue can impact their concentration, again resulting in unforced errors.

(4) To buy you time.

A defensive lob is useful when you are pulled wide and need time to return to a better court position or are tiring and want to slow down the game to catch your breath.

(5) To enable you to take the net

Having forced your opponent to retreat to the backcourt may present you with an opportunity to approach the net.

Once there, you become the aggressor and may have a chance to hit an easy winner.

Offensive Lob:

The offensive lob can be a powerful strategic tool against an aggressive net player, especially one who likes to crowd the net. It is hit high enough to clear your opponent's outstretched racquet, but not so high as to give them time to run back to make a return. When successfully executed, it can be an outright winner.

(Please see Figure 6.2)

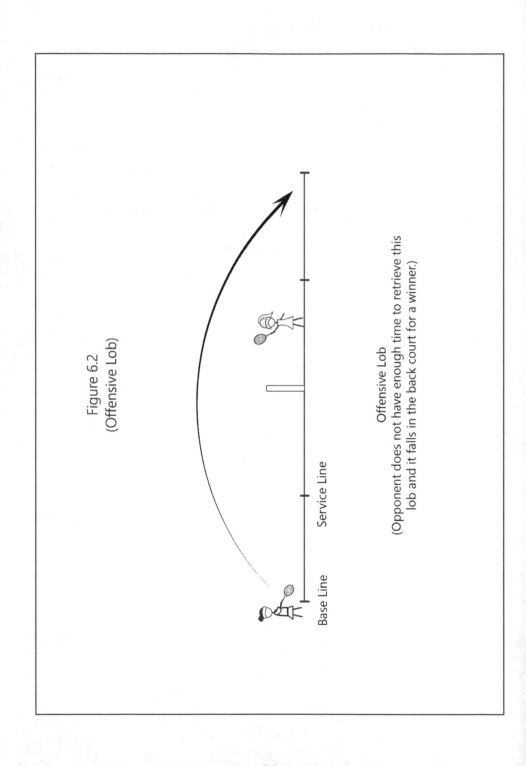

Figure 6.2
(Offensive Lob)

Base Line

Service Line

Offensive Lob
(Opponent does not have enough time to retrieve this
lob and it falls in the back court for a winner.)

Hitting an effective offensive lob is a bit more challenging than hitting a defensive one. It requires some finesse and preferably an ability to hit it with some topspin so that the ball drops quickly after passing over the opponent's outstretched racquet. (Successfully hitting a winning offensive lob is one of the more rewarding moments in the game.)

Even when you hit an offensive lob too high to be a winner, it forces your opponent away from the net. Like the defensive lob, it can:

- Take away their net advantage - at least for the moment
- Frustrate your opponent - resulting in a lapse in concentration
- Tire your opponent when done frequently in the match (Diabolical, no?)
- Provide an opportunity for you to take the net.

Where to hit lob:

Tip 1: **Strive to hit both types of lob to land in the backcourt (between the service line and the baseline) - the deeper, the better.**

A short lob that would bounce in the service court is trouble. It invites an overhead smash. (You may find it wise to duck!)

Tip 2: **Lob to your opponent's weakness.**

For most beginner and recreational players, this is their backhand side. Hitting an offensive lob to their backhand takes away the overhead smash. And it is generally more difficult to return -perhaps precipitating an unforced error.

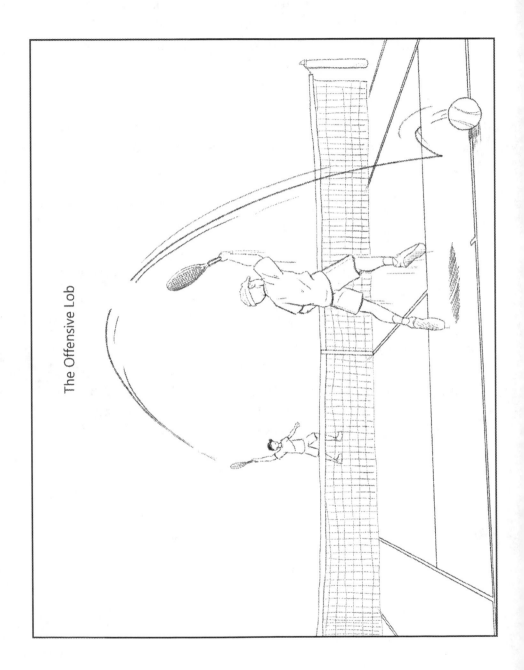

The Offensive Lob

CHAPTER 7

Poaching is Not a Crime!

Why Poach?

If you are playing doubles and not poaching, you are missing out on one of the ultimate forms of intimidation. Here's why.

- Poaching gives your team a psychological advantage, creating anxiety in the minds of your opponents. It is especially effective if you start poaching early in the match.
- Thinking you might poach at any time, your opponents may become uncertain about their service returns - perhaps causing a weak return or an unforced error.
- When the Receiver tries to keep one eye on the Server's partner at the net, they may mishit their return of serve, resulting in a weak return or an error.

If you and your doubles partner are not poaching, give it some thought. When you and your partner decide to poach, your mind focuses on hitting winners. The winner might be:

- an angled shot into the double's alley – out of reach of the opponent,
- a shot aimed at your opponent's feet, which they cannot return, or
- an untouchable volley crosscourt between your opponents. (Very cool!)

(Please see Figure 7.1)

Figure 7.1
The Poach

Some Tips for Successful Poaching:

Tip 1: **When to poach: Generally, on your partner's first serve.**

Since this is typically the more aggressive serve, it generally elicits a weaker return. Consequently, it offers favorable conditions for a successful poach.

Tip 2: **When to move: Ideally, just as the service Returner begins their stroke and is committed to their shot.**

- Better to move too early than too late. Your partner will be moving to cover your open court and should be able to get a down-the-line return.
- If you leave too late, you will not be able to cover a crosscourt return (unless you get lucky and the return is an easy sitter).

Tip 3: **Communicate your Intent**

- If you plan to poach, be sure to let your partner know - either verbally (between points) or with hand signals.
- Should you choose to communicate with hand signals, be consistent. Give a hand signal for every serve (e.g., open hand for going, fist for staying). If you only signal when you plan to poach, your partner will not be the only one who knows!

Tip 4: **Don't chicken out.**

- When you tell your partner you are going to go, go! Staying home will only give your opponent an open court for an easy winner! (And you'll have a frustrated partner.)

Tip 5:   **A fake poach is not unsportsmanlike**.

Making a move with your head or hips to suggest you are poaching is part of the game. When the Receiver sees you move your head or hips as if you were crossing, they may change their stroke at the last minute and make an error! (Imagine a point just for faking!)

Remember, the goal of a poach is to end the point with a winner. Hopefully, keeping this in mind will bolster your confidence to where poaching becomes a comfortable and vital part of your doubles strategy.

If you play doubles, and you and your partner are not poaching, give it a try. If at first, you don't succeed, don't be discouraged. Practice makes perfect!

CHAPTER 8

Let Your Feet 'Up' Your Game

At some time in your playing past, I expect you lost a few points because you could not get to the ball. Or you got to the ball but did not have enough time to prepare for your shot. (Rats#*&%^^!)

You may be able to avoid many of these situations with attention to some fundamental footwork that is relatively easy to master. Doing so will help you get to the ball faster and be better prepared to stroke the ball.

Tip 1:	When moving right or left, don't turn to run in the direction you wish to go. Instead, shuffle your feet side-to-side, keeping your body facing the net. This footwork is especially useful when moving relatively short distances.

(Please see Figure 8.1)

Figure 8.1
Shuffle Step (to the left)

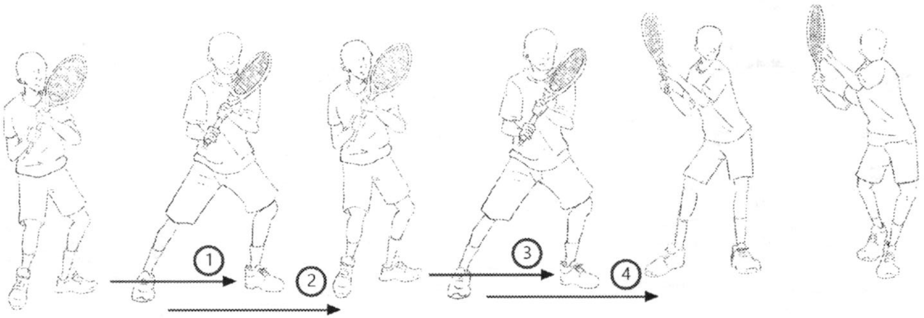

① Left foot slides to the left
② Right foot slides to the left
③ Left foot slides to the left
④ Right foot slides to the left

Doing so has several benefits.

- It allows you to cover more ground faster than turning and running, giving you more time to prepare for your shot.
- It allows you to keep your eyes on the ball as you move laterally across the court.
- If necessary, it allows you to stop and reverse direction faster than you could if you were running conventionally.
- It helps avoid being *wrong-footed* by your opponent.

Tip 2: **Stop moving before your opponent strikes the ball, coming to a balanced split-stop position.**

Doing so will:

- Enable you to react to your opponent's shot (whether right or left) and avoid being wrong-footed.
- Allow you to be in the ready position (balanced, eyes on your opponent, racquet out in front of your body.)

Tip 3. **When you need to cover a relatively long distance, start by first making a *crossover step*. For example, when going to your right, move your left foot across the right foot & leg, keeping your eyes on the ball as you move to intercept your opponent's return.**

Doing so enables you to cover the longer distance faster than the side-to-side shuffle step.

Notice that your racquet moves back when making this crossover step - saving you valuable preparation time when you intercept the ball.

(Please see Figure 8.2)

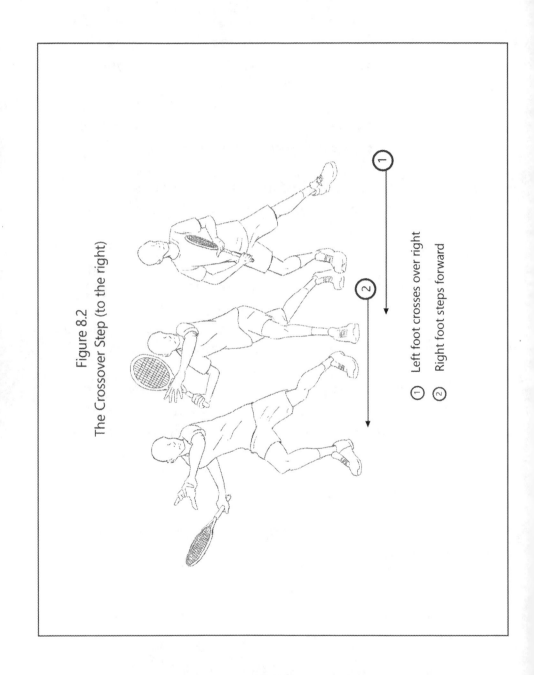

Figure 8.2
The Crossover Step (to the right)

① Left foot crosses over right
② Right foot steps forward

Once you get used to this footwork and movement, you will find you get to more of your opponent's shots. And are better prepared to make a good return.

CHAPTER 9

Bringing Out the Best in Your Doubles Partner

As a young player, I frowned upon doubles (probably because I was uncomfortable going to the net!) As I aged and could not be as agile or as quick as I was as a youth, I discovered doubles and instantly regretted not having done so sooner. Unlike singles, whose outcome is solely dependent upon each opponent, doubles is a team sport. And, by its nature is more sociable.

In doubles, you get to work with your partner, strategizing for a successful outcome. However, depending upon your demeanor, it can quickly become unpleasant. Here are a few tips that I trust will help you and your partner maintain the enjoyment of playing together.

Tip 1: **Never criticize or show disappointment (especially if your partner is your spouse!)**

If your partner has just made an unforced error, they already feel bad. Why make it worse. Criticism only further discourages them and gives your opposition a psychological lift. Remember, tennis is a *game of errors*. If you or your partner never missed, you would be *on the tour.*

| Tip 2: | **Be encouraging at every opportunity.** |

Say, "great shot!" "Nice lob!" "Good get!" "No problem, let's do it here." "It's alright; we'll get them on the next point." Let them know you appreciate their effort!

| Tip 3: | **Talk to one another between points.** |

Doing so allows you to be supportive, plan your next point, or get a breather. If nothing else, it will make your opponents wonder what you are planning! (Nice way to psych-out the opposition.)

| Tip 4: | **Communicate during the point.** |

- Remember to let your partner know if you plan to poach.
- If you need to switch sides, yell out, "Switch."
- If the opponents return the ball up the middle, call out "mine" or "yours" to let your partner know who should take the ball.
- Always be encouraging!

| Tip 5: | **Never change a winning strategy.** |

If the game you and your partner are playing is working, why change it?

| Tip 6: | **Always change a losing strategy.** |

If you are getting killed in the game you are playing, try something else.

For example, if you are not poaching, add it to your game the next time your team serves. If you're playing deuce court and your partner the ad court, switch at the start of the next set. If your opponents are lobbing you successfully, move back to the baseline, and wait for an opportunity to approach the net.

There's no guarantee the change will make a difference, but you have nowhere to go but up!

CHAPTER 10

Know Your Jobs in Doubles

Unlike singles, in which you wear all the hats, each doubles player has some specific responsibilities. Here we will deal with a summary of each player's duties during the serve. It's not rocket science, but merely a reminder to help you focus on your partner's expectations during the start of each point.

(Please see Figure 10.1)

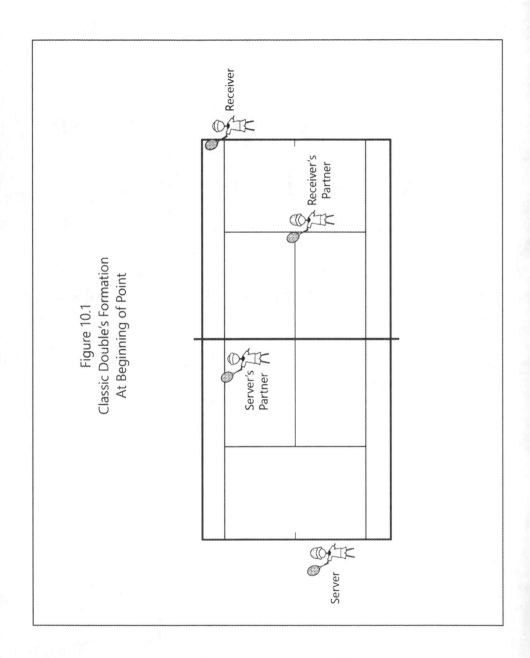

Figure 10.1
Classic Double's Formation
At Beginning of Point

Server's Responsibilities

- **Strive to get the first serve in play.**

  This is typically the more potent serve and the best potential to surprise - especially at the beginner level. (Surprise is good!)

- **Should your first serve be a fault, strive to get your second serve in play 90% of the time.**

  Be aggressive! And remember - double-faulting is not a sin!

- **Return the Receiver's return of service.**

  If they successfully returned your service, your obligation to your partner is to keep the ball in play. Give your opponents another opportunity to make an error!

- **Cover the *deep lob* as a return of serve.**

  Should the service Receiver hit a deep lob, move to a position to make the return. Since your partner is at the net (intent on making a winning volley), they would have to take their eyes off the ball to retreat into a position to make the return.

  You can do so without taking your eyes off the ball. (Make sense?)

  Your partner will move to the open court and join you in the defensive zone. Upon returning the deep lob, you both can then advance to the net together.

  (Please see Figure 10.2)

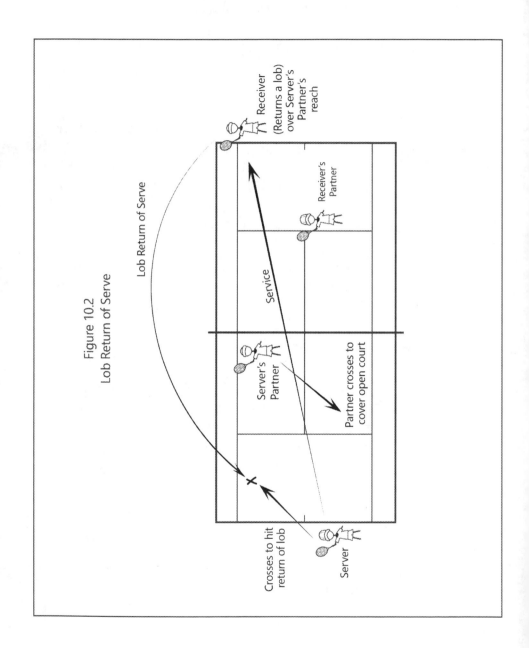

Figure 10.2
Lob Return of Serve

Lob Return of Serve

Receiver
(Returns a lob)
over Server's
Partner's
reach

Receiver's
Partner

Service

Server's
Partner

Partner crosses to
cover open court

Crosses to hit
return of lob

Server

- **Follow your serve to join your partner at the net.**

  If you and your partner have agreed to take the net, follow your serve's flight by taking a few steps forward. Remember to *split-step* before your opponent strikes the ball to give you the best chance of reacting to the next return.

Server's Partner Responsibilities

- **Intimidate the Receiver!**

  Be in a "ready" position about 6 feet from the net - balanced on the balls of your feet, racquet out in front of you, and eyes intently focused on your opponent receiving serve. Being ready will not only enable you to quickly respond to the service return if it comes in your direction but also may rattle the Receiver.

  If your attempt at intimidation is successful, it may cause your opponent to take their eyes off the ball or try extra hard to keep their return of serve away from you. In so doing, they may make an unforced error. (Your point! Yea!)

- **Be ready to put away a weak service return.**

  You are already in the *Kill Zone*. If you get a weak service return within your reach, put it away! (It's one of the more enjoyable shots in the game.)

Receiver's Responsibilities

- **Be in an optimal location to return the serve.**

  If you are confident in both your forehand and backhand, observe the Server's position and *bisect the angle* (Figure 10-3). Doing so gives you an equal opportunity to get to most serves.

  (Please see Figure 10.3)

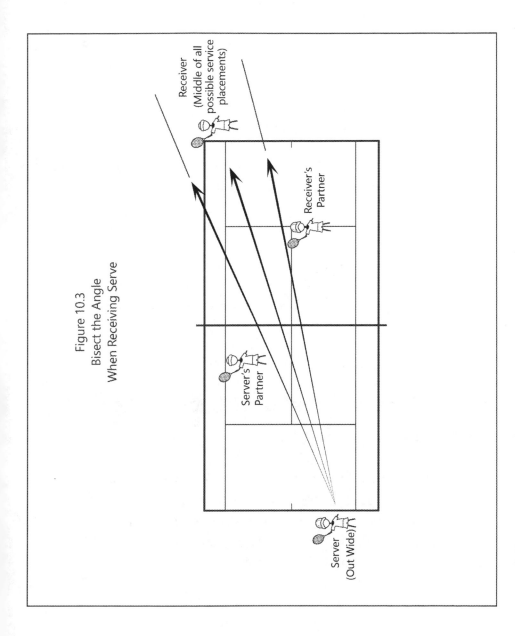

Figure 10.3
Bisect the Angle
When Receiving Serve

Receiver
(Middle of all
possible service
placements)

Receiver's
Partner

Server's
Partner

Server
(Out Wide)

- **Be in the *ready* position.**

  Be balanced on the balls of your feet, racquet out in front of you, eyes on the Server. Doing so gives you the best opportunity to move to the ball and suggests to the Server that you can handle whatever he sends your way. (Bring it on!)

- **Return the serve in play!**

  Make every effort to keep your return of the service away from the Server's partner at the net.

- **Call the serve "out" if it is deep or wide.**

  Tennis etiquette dictates that the receiving team be responsible for calling the service if it is out. After all, you are much closer to the landing point than the Server or their partner. (And remember, no line shrinking!)

Receiver's Partner Responsibilities

- **Be in the *ready* position.**

  Be balanced on the balls of your feet, racquet out in front of you, eyes on the Server, and just at or slightly inside the service line (perhaps, slightly favoring the middle of the court where the service Returner has the highest probability of avoiding a net error.)

  Doing so shows the opponents that you're ready to join the rally after the service return.

- **Call the serve "out" if it is deep or wide.**

  Tennis etiquette dictates that the receiving team be responsible for calling the service if it is out. (And again, no line shrinking!)

  (Please see Figure 10.4)

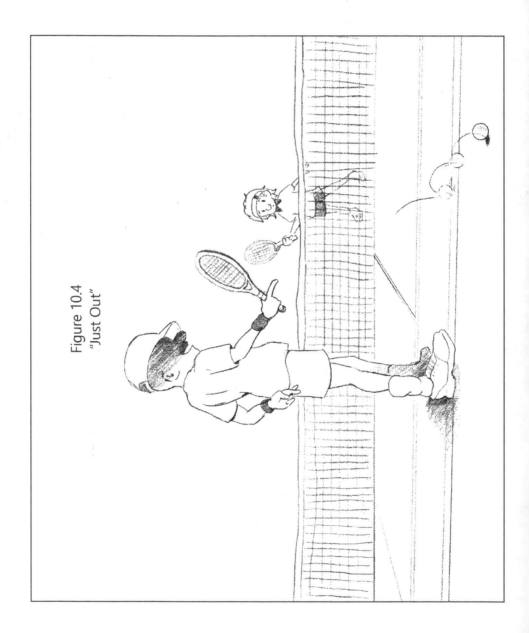

Figure 10.4
"Just Out"

CHAPTER 11

Choosing the Best Doubles Formation

When playing doubles, there are three basic formations from which partners typically choose to play. Let's have a quick review of the pros and cons of each.

Both Back Formation

Here both you and your partner hit groundstrokes from the Defensive Zone.

Pros:

- Both players can cover the middle of the court.
- Your team can get to most deep returns hit between the sidelines.
- It is difficult for the opponents to hit passing shots.
- It puts pressure on the opponents to hit winning wide-angled volleys or excellent drop shots.
- It takes the lob away from the opponents.
- It is a good formation if the Receiving team is aggressively attacking the Service and driving returns directly at the net player.

Cons:

- It is purely a defensive formation making it difficult to hit winners from the baseline.
- Your only offensive weapons are the drop shot (against opponents in the backcourt) or lobs (against opponents at the net).
- It is difficult to cover the forecourt against angled shots and drop volleys.
- It offers many angles for the opposing team to hit winning volleys at the net.

(Please see Figure 11.1)

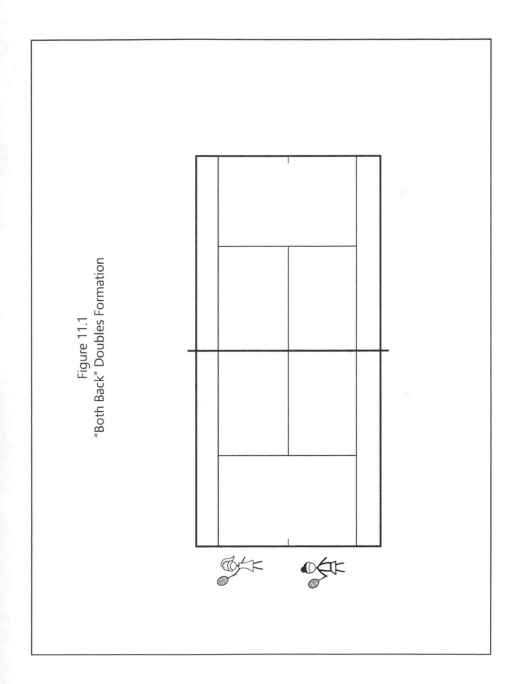

Figure 11.1
"Both Back" Doubles Formation

One Up, One Back Formation

Pros:

- One player (at the net) can play offensively- if the opportunity arises.
- It may be an effective strategy for a team with a strong baseliner and a competent net player.

Cons:

- It leaves the middle of the court (between the net and baseline players) open for easy winning volleys by the opponent(s) at the net. Of course, this disadvantage disappears if your opponents are both at the baseline.
- The baseline player has few options to play offensively, with a lob or perhaps a drop shot (if their opponent is deep).

(Please see Figure 11.2)

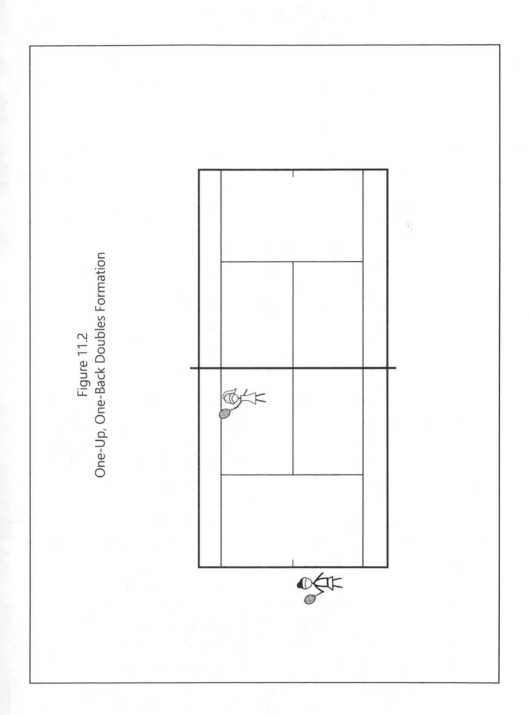

Figure 11.2
One-Up, One-Back Doubles Formation

Both Up Formation

Pros:

- It puts tremendous pressure on the opponents.
- Both players can cover the middle of the court.
- It is difficult for opponents to hit passing shots.
- Both players can play offensively - hitting winning volleys and overhead smashes.

Cons:

- Net players are susceptible to the lob.
- It is hard to move back to retrieve defensive lobs.

(Please see Figure 11.3)

Which Formation is Best?

In highly competitive tennis, the answer to this question is generally – both up.

Here both players are on offense, in command of the net, and can direct winning volleys at many angles to an open area of the court.

However, at the beginner or intermediate level, your choice may depend upon several variables? These include, but are not limited to:

- What formation is your opponent using?
- How comfortable are you and your partner at the net?
- How capable are you and your partner at the net?
- How competent are your opponents at the net?
- How strong are your opponents' groundstrokes?
- How strong are your opponents' return of serve?

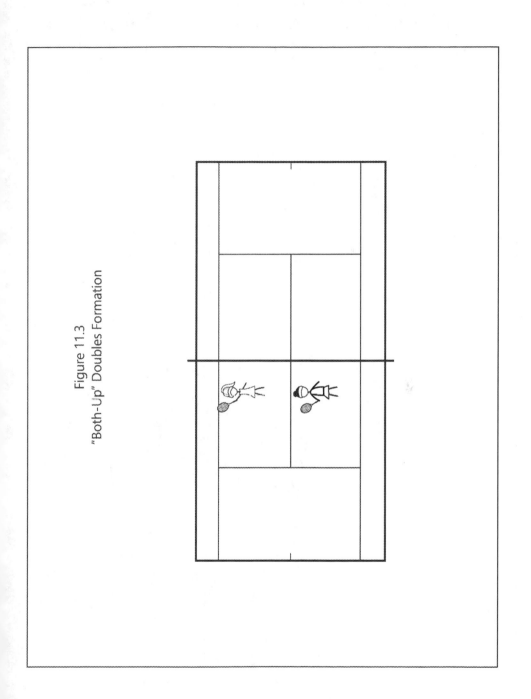

Figure 11.3
"Both-Up" Doubles Formation

In the final analysis, I would encourage you to choose the formation that suits your and your partner's personality, style of play, and strengths. And remember, you can change your doubles look at any time as the match progresses.

Whatever your decision and the outcome – it is just a game. (Enjoy!)

CHAPTER 12

Foreplay: Tips to Intimidate your Opponent Before the Match Begins

Since this book is meant to help you have more fun on the court, it seemed appropriate to share a few pre-match tips which might help give you a psychological edge on your opponent before the match begins. And possibly help you play better. (Wouldn't that be nice!)

I trust some of them may make you smile and muse, "Why didn't I think of that! Hopefully, some will resonate with you and become a regular part of your pre-match warm-up.

<u>Before the Warm-Up</u>

Tip 1: Bring 1 (or even 2) extra racquets.

These extra racquets need not be strung! Just be sure the racquet heads each have a cover or are inside your tennis bag with only the grips visible. They will make you look like a 'seasoned' veteran - someone who has come to play ... no matter what!

(Please see Figure 12.1)

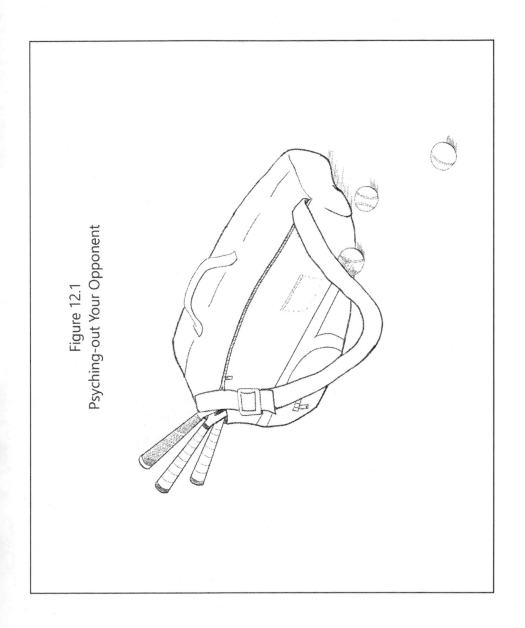

Figure 12.1
Psyching-out Your Opponent

Tip 2: Dress like a tennis player.

No Bermuda shorts, muscle shirts, or black socks! Dressing appropriately makes an unconscious statement that you are a player. It's also an interesting phenomenon to note that (often) if you dress the part, you'll subconsciously feel the part. And probably play better.

Tip 3: Do some mild stretching before you start the warm-up.

Knee bends, trunk rotations, waist bends, etc. Doing so will give the opponent the impression that you are limber and ready for anything they offer. Just another psychological signal that you are serious about playing. And, if you are loose and relaxed, you will play at your best.

Tip 4: If you're proficient at this, try bouncing the ball in the center of your racquet strings while your opponent is preparing for the warm-up.

This simple exercise is great for your concentration. It will also signal that you have excellent racquet control and good eye-hand coordination - two critical elements for consistent play.

During the Warm-Up

Tip 5: Don't run to return shots that are wide (out of play).

It isn't easy to correctly set up when on the run. Without proper set-up, you'll make unforced errors, giving your opponent confidence in your inability to return the ball consistently.

Besides, all that running for their errant returns only tires you out before actual play begins. Why make their error, your error? Just let them go, drop another ball, and continue the warm-up. (They will know you did not return it because it was out – perhaps putting a small dent in their confidence.)

Tip 6: Don't run in to hit their short shots on a single bounce.

While it will be necessary to do so during the match, doing so during the warm-up has the same drawbacks as hitting their "wide" returns. Instead, let these short balls come to you at the baseline, prepare, and hit an excellent, controlled return.

Tip 7: Never hit any shots that are going to land behind the baseline.

Letting them bounce deep emphasizes that your opponent's shot was long – causing them a little frustration each time this occurs. (Yes!)

Also, trying to hit these long balls on-the-fly or with a half-volley is difficult and likely to result in you making an error. (And we want to avoid that as often as possible.)

Tip 8: Show them your game!

If you can, hit forehands, backhands, lobs, overheads, volleys, and serves - all with control. Try not to telegraph any weakness during the warm-up. If you do, they will surely use it to their advantage during match play. (Ugh!)

Tip 9: Don't show emotion during the warm-up.

Don't get upset if you mishit, put the ball in the net, or hit an "out" ball. Stay calm. Drop another ball and continue the warm-up. Remember, tennis is a game of errors. Making one is simply a part of the game, not something to get upset about!

Tip 10: Most importantly, concentrate on each of your strokes during the warm-up! Focus on controlling each return and keeping the ball in play.

Doing so will result in the most favorable impression of your ability – and will carry forward during match play.

One Final Tip:

Remember that tennis is a game of errors. If you never missed, you would be on the pro tour gathering fame and for fortune.

Have fun!

ABOUT THE AUTHOR

Peter is a USPTA Registered Elite Professional. An alumnus of Vic Braden's Tennis College, he has spent more than 35 years playing, learning, teaching, and enjoying this incredible sport. During this time, he has accumulated several strategic, tactical, and psychological tips he believes may help recreational players elevate their game and, more importantly, heighten their level of enjoyment. It is his hope that readers will enjoy and benefit from these practical, and sometimes lighthearted, tips.

L

Printed in the United States
by Baker & Taylor Publisher Services